LIVING FOR THE *FUTURE*

BUSINESS AND INDUSTRY

Simon Beavis and Chris Barrie

W
FRANKLIN WATTS
NEW YORK • LONDON • SYDNEY

Most of our everyday activities, whether turning on a light or taking a trip in a car, use up some of the earth's resources. These resources will not last forever, yet we continue to need and use them in our daily lives.

In June 1992, the largest ever political meeting in history was held – the United Nations Conference on Environment and Development (UNCED), or the 'Earth Summit'. Politicians, environmental experts and many others gathered together to discuss the challenge that humanity faces as we move towards the twenty-first century. How can we live our lives in a way that suits us, but without using up the resources that our children in turn will need to live their lives?

Agenda 21 is the document that was produced as a result of the Earth Summit. It sets out a practical plan for every nation to follow to achieve 'sustainable development'. This means not only allowing ourselves to live the lives we want to lead, but allowing everyone else to live a comfortable life, while also protecting our environment for future generations.

For Dario, Alida, Laura, Jessica, Thomas, Gabriel and William

© 1998 Franklin Watts
96 Leonard Street
London
EC2A 4RH

Franklin Watts Australia
14 Mars Road
Lane Cove
NSW 2066

ISBN 0 7496 3017 5

Dewey Decimal Classification Number 363.7

A CIP catalogue record for this book is available from the British Library

Series editor: Helen Lanz
Series designer: Kirstie Billingham
Designer: Simon Borrough
Picture research: Sue Mennell
Consultant: Niall Marriott, a founder of Living Earth Foundation and consultant in environmental, community and educational issues

Printed in the United Kingdom

Picture credits
Cover images: Front cover: Robert Harding (Robert Francis/main image), Still Pictures (Dylan Garcia); Backcover: Still Pictures (Mark Edwards).

Inside image: BirdLife, FFI and BP (by the team of Sangihe-Talaud Conservation Project) 27b; Clarks International 11b; Ecoscene 5t (Barry Webb); ©1992 GM Corp. Used with permission GM Media Archives. 21t; Robert Harding Picture Library 17t (Liaison Int.), 20m; Hutchison Library 6t (Felix Greene), 7r (Bernard Regent), 16b (Philip Wolmuth), 17b (Robert Francis),22t (J.A. Horner); Panos Pictures 4b (Jeremy Hartley), 9t (Guiseppe Bizzari), 12t (Ron Giling), 16t (Sean Sprague), 18t (R. Giling), 19t (Trgyve Bolstad), 19b (Chris Stowers), 22b (Ingrid Morato), 23b (Sean Sprague), 24t (Nancy Durrell McKenna), 25t (Sean Sprague), 25b (Guy Mansfield), 26t (Gisele Wulfsohn), 26b (Ron Giling), 27t (Liba Taylor), 29b (Penny Tweedie); Popperfoto/Reuters (Michael Urban), 9b (Kamal Kishore); Saab Automobile AB 20t; Sony UK Ltd. 15b; Still Pictures 4t (Mark Edwards), 5b (David Hoffman), 6b (Heldur Metocny), 7l (David Drain), 8t (Michel Gunther), 10t (Mark Edwards), 10b (Hartmut Schwarzbach), 11t (Peter Frischmuth), 12b (Mark Edwards), 14t (Mark Edwards), 14b (Thomas Raupach), 15t (Mauri Raukari, 18b (Mark Edwards), 20b (Harmut Schwarzbach), 21b (Julio Etchart, 23t (Mark Edwards) 24b (Mark Edwards), 28t (Mark Edwards) 28b (EIA, Peru), 29t (Mark Cawardine) 29m (Peter Frischmuth); Times Newspapers Ltd. 13 (Simon Walker).

CONTENTS

Factories, mines, building sites, banks and shops are all part of business and industry. They play a vital role in the societies in which we live. They provide people with jobs and wages allowing them to support themselves and their families.

Factories create wealth, but also add to pollution.

INDUSTRY: THE GOOD AND THE BAD

THE BENEFITS OF BUSINESS

Services (such as advice from banks on how to invest money) and goods (the products sold in shops) can be bought by local people and can also be sold abroad. This adds to the wealth of the country providing them. Additionally, most businesses pay taxes to their country's government. This money helps to pay for other services such the schools and hospitals on which we all rely.

Trade, the buying and selling of goods, helps create wealth for a country.

WASTE AND POLLUTION

But industry does not just provide good things. Even though it can help to improve our lives, it can also cause damage. It has a huge appetite for resources such as trees, water, gas, oil and coal. Careless industries can leave huge areas of the earth devastated and threaten human, animal and plant life. It creates waste which, if not dealt with responsibly, can leave the land, sea and air polluted.

The earth is full of precious resources such as coal, which are burned to create heat, power and light. But resources don't last forever.

'An increasing amount of hazardous waste is affecting human health and the environment.'

AGENDA 21

A RECKLESS PAST

For nearly 200 years, the richest countries in the world, such as those in Western Europe and Australasia, and the United States, have built powerful industries. But they have only recently started worrying about the environment. Poorer, developing countries are now trying to catch up. They want a share in the wealth that industry can bring.

THE ROLE OF BUSINESS

Business and industry are recognized by governments as a way for people to earn a wage and so gain a good standard of living. But, increasingly, governments are realizing that each country needs to offer a better way of life for its citizens without causing environmental damage and human suffering.

Dangerous waste is carefully removed. Developing countries do not always appreciate being told to be careful about industrial pollution when they know countries in the West were reckless in the past.

Energy is needed to provide people with heat and light in their homes and places of work. It is also needed to produce the many products that the world's industries make. Fuels such as coal, oil and gas are burned to provide industry with the power it needs to create electricity and to provide all the goods that people have come to expect. But creating and using all this power has a cost.

Steel production uses huge amounts of energy.

THE IMPACT OF INDUSTRY

THE COST OF FUEL

The world digs up 3 billion tonnes of coal a year and in doing so shifts some 15 billion tonnes of earth, rock and water. When the coal is burned it creates 10 billion tonnes of carbon dioxide (CO_2). The CO_2 helps create a layer in the atmosphere which traps the earth's heat, causing the world temperature to rise. This is known as 'global warming' or the 'greenhouse effect'. Global warming causes storms, droughts and floods which can destroy large areas or even countries, forcing millions of people to leave their homes.

Floods caused by global warming threaten areas such as Bangladesh.

In developed countries, industry is directly responsible for creating about 50% of CO_2 emissions.

THE LOSS OF FORESTS

Industry is responsible for affecting the environment in many ways. Huge areas of forests are cleared each year to provide wood for burning, or for making paper or building materials. Trees are also cut down to make way for roads or to provide more farm land. But woods and deep forests are vital for keeping the atmosphere clean: trees absorb CO_2 and turn it into the oxygen we breathe. Trees help keep the land intact: when dense forests are cleared, the soil tends to be thin and unfertile. It is easily blown away, creating dust bowls and deserts.

Short-term gain of clearing forests to make products such as paper results in the long-term loss of an important natural resource.

AIR AND WATER POLLUTION

Smoke from industrial chimneys contains waste gases such as nitrogen and sulphur oxides. These gases poison rain clouds and create acid rain. This often falls hundreds of kilometres from the original factory that produced the pollution. Land, rivers and lakes become poisoned and useless.

Nuclear power stations create fewer emissions than traditional power stations, but they produce other harmful by-products such as radiation.

Another cause for concern is other waste gases from industry that affect the 'ozone layer' which surrounds the earth. This layer is a thin gas screen about 25 km above the earth's surface. It shields the earth from harmful ultra-violet (UV) rays, but lets through the sunlight which is needed by plants and humans.

'Governments should put into force international agreements calling for reductions in the use of ozone depleting substances.'

AGENDA 21

The destruction of the ozone layer allows more of the sun's UV rays to reach the earth, causing cancer.

DUMPING WASTE

Traditionally, industry has been careless about the waste it makes and its disposal, dumping it in landfill sites, rivers and the sea. Some countries are introducing tough laws to cut down waste, but others remain lax. Sometimes companies will transport waste to neighbouring countries (where the rules are less strict than their own) in order to dump waste.

Nuclear waste is so dangerous it has to be sealed in special containers. It takes hundreds of years to become safe.

People are an important resource too and need to be looked after.

But the damage caused by industry is not all done to the environment. Just as industry makes demands on the environment, it also asks a lot of the people who work in it.

As the world population increases, there is a shortage of work. This means that companies can get people who are desperate for a job to work for them for little money, possibly in poor or unsafe conditions. In countries without proper employment laws, it is the most vulnerable who are taken advantage of: companies often find the cheapest labour to be poor women or children.

CASE STUDY

BHOPAL, INDIA

THE TRAGEDY OF BHOPAL

In the early morning darkness of December 3, 1984, a cloud of poisonous gas drifted out of a chemical factory in the Indian town of Bhopal. By dawn, 8,000 men, women and children had died in their houses and on the streets. Another 12,000 people died later, with as many as 200,000 people suffering ill-affects. It was one of the world's worst industrial disasters.

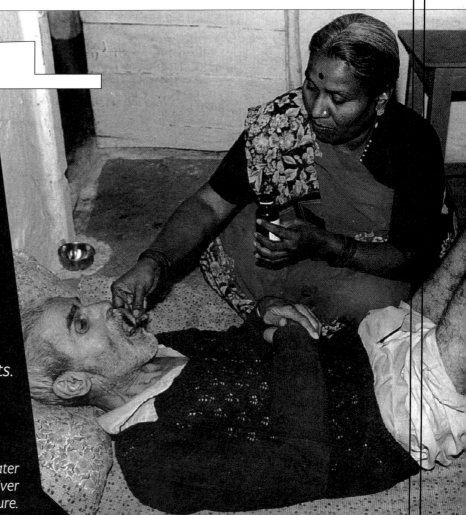

Many survivors of the Bhopal disaster later became ill, suffering blindness as well as liver and kidney failure.

As it became clear that the earth is being damaged and the poor countries are staying poor, a meeting was called to agree on how to solve these problems. In June 1992, leaders and representatives from 178 governments met in Rio de Janeiro at the 'United Nations Conference on Environment Development' or the 'Earth Summit'. They agreed to follow a plan called Agenda 21, which is a practical guide to a better future.

The Earth Summit was a huge event.

GOALS FOR THE FUTURE

CLEAR GOALS

Agenda 21 looks at almost every way that people affect the environment. It sets out clear goals, making sure that people can enjoy a good lifestyle and standard of living, whilst also making sure that future generations can enjoy a comfortable lifestyle too. This is called 'sustainable development'.

Nepal is a long way from heavy industry. But if we want to enjoy even the remotest places, industry has to be more careful.

Although Agenda 21 is not a law – no one has to follow it – governments and companies can never again damage the environment and say, as an excuse, that they did not know what they ought to be doing. More than that, for the first time the whole world has agreed that the earth matters, and that it is in danger.

German experts make sure no radiation escapes from this nuclear cargo. Industry is being forced to clean up its mess.

'A large part of conservation, resource use, waste reduction, rights of workers . . . lies in the hands of businessmen.'

Rescue Mission Planet Earth, children's edition of Agenda 21.

A SENSE OF RESPONSIBILITY

Changing the way b...ss works is vital if Ag... is to be a succ... have a gre... peopl... In s... ind... lik... t...

C&J. CLARK STREET, Somersetshire.

C&J. CLARK, STREET, SOMERSET. ESTABLISHED. TRADE MARK

Prize Medal

MANUFACTURERS OF
Gentlemen's Children's **BOOTS, SHOES & SLIPPERS,** Fair Wear Guaranteed.

In the 1880s, Clarks, the shoemaker, provided work <u>and</u> moral guidance for the people of Street in England. In the 1990s, many still depended on Clarks and were shocked at the loss of 330 jobs.

Some companies have taken Agenda 21 very seriously. But others have not. One problem is that many businesses are only interested in making money — it is often cheaper to continue with the old, polluting industrial methods, rather than go to the expense of installing newer, cleaner technology.

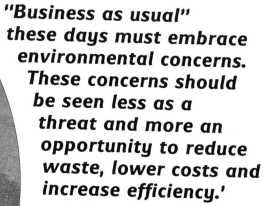

In Mexico, factory pollution matters less than having work.

' "Business as usual" these days must embrace environmental concerns. These concerns should be seen less as a threat and more an opportunity to reduce waste, lower costs and increase efficiency.'

Environment Forum newsletter, 1996.

...er ...hemicals.

Most businesses will not alter until they are forced to change the way they work. When industry has to pay to clean up the pollution it creates, for example, or when the public start to buy someone else's products that are made in a more environmentally-sensitive way, then industrial practices will change.

Here are some of the most important aims of Agenda 21 to achieve sustainable business and industry:

- industry must produce goods using as little energy as possible, recycling materials and using renewable resources where possible
- industry must work to protect air quality by cutting the amount of pollution and waste
- chemicals and toxic wastes must be handled carefully
- richer, developed countries must help developing countries by transferring 'clean' technology and by paying them a fair price for their goods

13

CASE STUDY

GLOBAL ISSUES

EARTH SUMMIT II

Environmental issues are still high on the agenda for many countries. Governments realize that issues such as global warming are now scientific fact. Major changes to the way we live our lives still need to be made.

In June 1997, five years on from the Rio Summit, Earth Summit II was held in New York. This assessed the progress made in achieving the aims of Agenda 21. It found that Germany and Britain are likely to meet the targets set at the original Earth Summit, to control green-house gas emissions. But this is only one of the issues and just two countries from across the world. There is still much to do.

The United States came under much criticism at Earth Summit II. It produces 20% of the world's carbon emissions, but will not commit to reducing this level.

- promote the efficient use of raw materials
- encourage companies to assess how they affect the environment
- promote the use of safe, cheap, clean transport systems

Trees are used in vast numbers.

A RAW DEAL

Iron ore is used to make steel or aluminium for cars and planes.

All companies rely on the earth's resources for basic raw materials: metals, gas, coal, oil, water, sand and wood. Few industries can do much without these in either their natural form or after they have been refined into something else. Oil, for example, is used to provide energy for other products such as petrol or plastic; sand is used to make glass for windows.

DAMAGE

The earth has always been rich in natural resources. These resources, many of which have developed over centuries, cannot be replaced. They are non-renewable. Now some of the earth's most important resources are running out. Additionally, digging them out of the ground causes huge amounts of waste, damage and pollution.

MAKING A DIFFERENCE

We need to save resources. That means gathering them more carefully, reducing the demand for them and using renewable resources that do not run out – such as the sun, the wind, water or wave power. Companies can make a big difference by carefully checking what they use and by finding less wasteful ways of manufacturing their products.

Replacing resources where possible, such as replanting trees, is a sustainable way to work.

An average family car weighs only 1 tonne. To get the materials to make it and to put them all together, some 15 tonnes of solid waste is created.

CASE STUDY

SONY ACROSS THE GLOBE

SONY'S GREEN TV

The Japanese company Sony has designed an advanced 'green' TV which is nearly 25 per cent lighter than older sets and cuts the amount of plastic it uses by half. Important parts of the TV sets can be recycled: to ensure that people take advantage of this feature, Sony have used clip-on or slide-in parts rather than awkward screws and glues.

Like Sony, other hi-tech companies are realizing they can benefit from better design and recycling.

THE COST OF TRANSPORT

Industry has to transport its goods to the places where they are sold. Some goods are moved small distances, while others are carried many thousands of kilometres. But lorries, cars, planes and ships create huge pollution. Transport creates more nitrogen oxide (one of the worst acid rain gases) than factories. It also uses up many non-renewable fuels.

Petrol – refined from oil – is not the only thing that can power cars. Yet, despite the fact that oil is running out, petrol is still by far the most commonly used fuel the world over.

'Growing congestion on UK roads is making freight transport by lorry more unreliable and environmentally less desirable than rail transport.'

English, Welsh & Scottish Railways.

16

Efficient transport systems are vital, as are well-maintained modern vehicles which do not belch out fumes or use too much petrol. But building modern transport systems is expensive. The world's richest nations find it hard enough to find the money. In developing countries, the bill is often just too huge to manage.

Ports in Britain have become more efficient. But congestion and pollution remain problems.

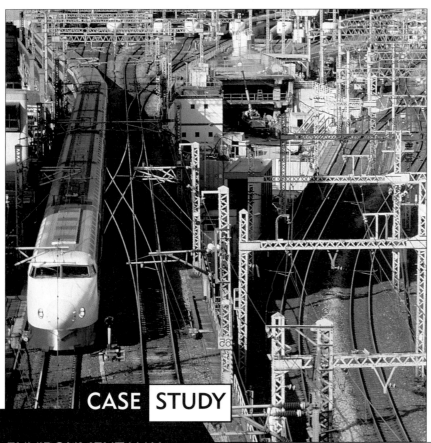

EXISTING SYSTEMS

Companies should look at whether they could cut down on journeys that are not necessary. Additionally, they should make better use of existing transport systems that are more environmentally sensitive than transporting goods by road.

In many countries there is space on railways for more goods. But unless rail becomes cheaper, companies will use lorries instead.

CASE STUDY

ENVIRONMENTALLY-
SENSITIVE TRANSPORT

THE VALUE OF THE RAILWAYS

In recent years, the quantity of freight being moved by road has increased. The more companies use lorries to transport their products, the cheaper this method of transport becomes. The amount of pollution in the air, however, goes up.

Rail was the traditional method of moving freight. There are existing rail lines in developed and developing countries alike. Rail causes less pollution, less congestion on the roads and is more environmentally sensitive.

Most freight in Britain goes by road but the government wants to return to rail and barges.

AGENDA 21 aims to:

- cut industrial pollution and waste and promote recycling
- encourage the sharing of technology to make processes cleaner
- promote the use of safer chemicals
- prevent the dumping of waste in developing countries

Chinese industry is booming.

WHAT A WASTE

Developed countries used to be relaxed about the pollution and waste that their industries produced. Fumes from coal-burning fires in homes combined with the pollution from factories and created 'smogs' – dense fog that made people choke.

TOXIC WASTE

In 1988 an Italian company tried to dump dangerously toxic waste on a beach in Nigeria. The waste was rejected and the load was sent to many European countries which also refused to take it. Eventually, it was dealt with in Italy. Careless dumping of waste or off-loading it in developing countries is not allowed under Agenda 21.

Smogs are caused by pollution from cars and industry. Today they are becoming less common.

CLEAN PRODUCTS, LESS WASTE

Industry in developed countries is now much cleaner than it was; many countries now have laws limiting the fumes that factories and power stations can give off. Some businesses have also come to realize that making products cleanly can make them more money because less energy is wasted.

By using 'greener' working procedures, many companies find they can expand their business.

BUILDING UP INDUSTRIES IN DEVELOPING COUNTRIES

Developing countries want to make more goods. This will produce more pollution. In 1990, China and India contributed a third of carbon dioxide emissions. In the next 10 years they will be responsible for the fastest growth in greenhouse gas fumes. Tackling this problem concerns all countries.

In the 1990s, industry in Taiwan (above), China, India, Indonesia, South Korea and Thailand produced about a third of the world's goods. Experts believe they will account for over half the world trade by the year 2020.

INCREASING EFFICIENCY

Industry can cut down its use of energy and the level of pollution it creates by using renewable energy sources. Machines can be made more efficient, so that they use less energy to make their products.

Some 10 billion light bulbs are sold each year. At the moment, only one in 50 are longer-life, energy-efficient bulbs even though these new forms of lighting save huge amounts of power. There are now firms producing these new bulbs – first developed in the Netherlands – all over the world, including Eastern Europe and China.

MONITORING PROCESSES

Another way of cutting pollution is for companies to monitor their own processes. All industries depend on other companies supplying them with raw materials. More and more companies are realizing the importance of using suppliers that have good reputations: a poor supplier can damage the main company's image. For example, the Swedish car and aircraft maker, Saab, checks out all its suppliers before giving them work.

This Swedish car factory tries to look after its workforce as well as the environment.

'Measures should be taken to reduce industry's impact on the environment and to develop cleaner production methods.'

AGENDA 21

A RELUCTANCE TO CHANGE

Industry is often reluctant to change its processes because it is expensive to do so. Usually, it is only when industry cannot avoid updating its procedures that changes are made. It was only when the manmade gases, CFCs, used in goods such as fridges and aerosals, were found to be damaging the ozone layer that industry invested money in research to find alternative gases that could be used.

Production processes can be slow to change, but industries must accept their responsibilities.

America's biggest car companies are trying to make cars that are so light that they use only a fraction of the energy needed to power today's vehicles.

THE ROLE OF RESEARCH

An important part of industry is its 'research and development' programmes. Companies have to research making new products so they continue to produce goods that people will want to buy. This is a good opportunity for companies to consider products that will not only sell well, but will also be environmentally sensitive. In this way, the effect industry has on the environment will gradually be more and more positive.

CASE STUDY

GREENPEACE –
LEADING BY EXAMPLE

THE GREENFREEZE

Greenpeace – one of the leading organizations campaigning for a better environment – set about showing how industry could make products without using harmful chemicals. They helped develop a fridge, called a Greenfreeze, which used natural fuels as a coolant, rather than dangerous gases that were affecting the environment.

Chemical companies making traditional fridges said the idea would not work, but slowly the Greenfreeze won support. German fridge manufacturers were impressed with the idea; there was also huge interest in China where Greenfreeze fridges are now in production. There has been backing, too, in India, Pakistan, Kenya, Ghana and many parts of Latin America.

'Green' fridges help save the environment and provide work.

All farmers need a fair price for their produce.

TRADE AND DEBT

Poor countries feel pressure from the West to mine cheaply for raw materials.

People, companies and countries buy and sell products to one another to provide what we all need to live. Goods are usually sold at a profit (bringing in more money than the cost of making the products), so the companies and people selling the goods become richer.

Industrial nations, such as those in Western Europe and Australasia, and North America, have highly developed methods of manufacturing goods. While many industries in developing countries use more and more modern technology, some still rely on the country's natural riches. Mining precious metals, such as copper, or growing coffee or tea, are important sources of income.

A FAIR DEAL?

Often poorer countries, which have fewer products to sell, get low prices for their items, while richer countries charge more. This causes a 'trade gap' between developing and developed countries – poorer nations are trapped into staying poor.

AGENDA 21 aims to:

- promote fair trade
- allow developing countries to sell their goods freely and lessen their debts
- ensure new technology is transferred to developing countries

TAKING ADVANTAGE

Instead of helping, sometimes companies in developed nations take advantage of the situation in developing nations. Here, labour is much cheaper than in the West: companies use people from the poorer countries to make their products, paying them little.

Some international companies employ children in India who are as young as seven. They pay them only 6p an hour.

The world's poorest 48 countries have a tiny share of world trade and it is falling. If world trade was 300 big containers full of goods travelling on a ship, only one would belong to those 48 countries – and it would not even be full.

A MATTER OF SURVIVAL

Many of the poorer countries cannot afford the latest 'green' technology. When people are fighting to earn enough money to feed themselves, worrying about damaging the environment is not a high concern. But trade can help.

CREATING JOBS

Sometimes companies set up new factories abroad. It might be cheaper to build overseas, or managers may decide to set up a factory in the country where products sell particularly well. This creates new jobs and wealth in the 'host' country.

Without work the most vulnerable, such as this Brazilian mother and child, have to beg.

A GROWING DEBT

Sometimes poorer, developing nations need to borrow money from the richer ones. They are then often forced to produce certain goods for developed countries to pay off these debts. Agenda 21 says that it is the responsibility of the richer nations to pay enough to make sure that the poorer countries are able to look after their people and their region of the world.

Richer, developed nations can help poorer ones by buying their products for fair prices, regardless of any debts owed. This may mean richer countries have to pay more than they like for some products.

Developing countries have been bound by developed nations to grow crops as a way of paying off debts. This restricts the freedom of the poorer countries to earn money through trade and can contribute to keeping that country poor.

IMPROVING CONDITIONS

Trade can be used to encourage companies to treat people better and to adopt clean technology. Some Western organizations, such as the charity Oxfam, encourage local firms in poorer countries to improve working conditions by promising to pay a better price for the goods that these firms produce.

Factories providing well-paid jobs may need to charge more for their products.

'Cutting the debts of the world's 20 poorest countries would cost about $5.5 billion. That's less than it cost to build Disneyland in Paris.'

UN Human Development Report, 1997.

Projects which support fair trade and better working conditions are backed by the Fairtrade Foundation. Fairtrade is convinced that developing countries should gain independence from donations and loans from the West by being allowed to trade on fair terms in the goods which they themselves choose to produce.

Guarantees a **better deal** for Third World Producers

Fairtrade

CASE STUDY

SOUTHERN INDIA

LOOK AT THE LABEL

Shiragami works in Southern India as a tea picker. She is 36 years old and works six days a week. Unlike many others in her country, she has a contract and earns enough pay to support herself and her family. The estate provides loans and pays her when she is on maternity leave.

Because of these working conditions, the estate is approved by the Fairtrade Foundation. Packets of tea from this and other Fairtrade estates carry the Fairtrade Mark (above), so customers know that they are supporting a good company when they buy its tea.

Fairtrade gives Southern Indian tea pickers a better deal.

AGENDA 21 aims to:

- make people aware that they can influence business
- promote partnerships between business and environmental organizations
- promote the value of fair trade

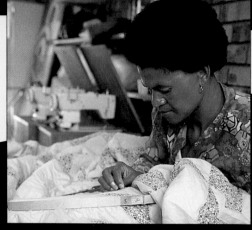

Agenda 21 helps people help themselves.

PARTNERSHIPS

Trade used to be thought a good idea for everyone and was encouraged. But there are problems. Trade can harm the world by encouraging people to make products or use up precious materials without thinking about the long-term damage to the environment.

Cooperation in and between businesses and environmental agencies is crucial.

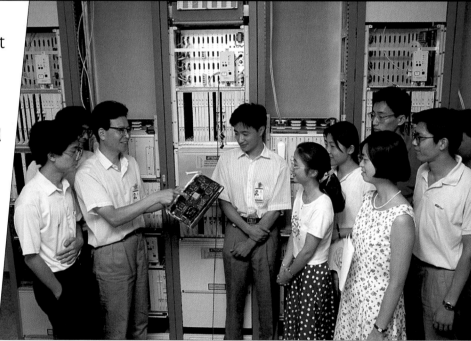

'The courage and ideals of the youth of the world should be used to forge a global partnership in order to achieve sustainable development and ensure a better future for all.'

AGENDA 21

PARTNERSHIPS

Sustainable development is only possible if everyone works together. Changes can be made by people working towards common goals. In business this means everybody matters – managers, workers, suppliers, owners and customers alike. In world terms, developed nations should help poor ones improve lifestyles, while protecting the environment.

All countries have a responsibility to keep assessing the way that they use the environment. Today, a business has three responsibilities: to make money in order to stay in business; to protect the environment on which most businesses depend for their raw materials; and to protect the people who work for them and who buy their services and products.

In this nursery in Ghana, farmers tend new trees. Good farming means nurturing new growth.

CASE STUDY

BRITAIN

A PARTNERSHIP BETWEEN BUSINESS AND THE ENVIRONMENT

General understanding and public awareness of 'green issues' has grown to the point that businesses now need to take account of the effect their practices have on the environment.

British Petroleum Company (BP) recognizes its responsibilities to the environment. It has joined the conservation organizations Fauna and Flora International and BirdLife International in supporting conservation projects and research around the world.

The research can be used by companies to help them clean up the way they work, reducing the pollution and destruction of the environment.

BP takes its environmental responsibilities seriously. Here it backs a scheme to help protect a rare bird.

Governments can guide business and industry in how they work by putting taxes on companies that pollute, or by calling for higher prices on products that harm the environment. But sometimes governments are frightened of doing this because they fear they will lose support.

'If 7 billion people were to consume as much as they do in the West today, we would need 10 worlds, not one, to satisfy these needs.'

Elizabeth Dowdeswell, a Canadian environmental expert.

New European laws have forced coal-fired power stations to install special pollution-reducing equipment.

Public concern over the danger of tuna nets forced a change in fishing methods. Consumer pressure does help.

Ordinary people can make a difference to how businesses behave. If a product is shown to damage the environment, people can stop buying it. For example, many people were horrified to find out that the Bottle-nosed Dolphin was in danger of being wiped out.

Many of the dolphins were trapped in nets used by fishermen trying to catch tuna for us to eat. People protested by not buying tuna caught in the nets that also trapped dolphins. Now new ways of catching tuna have been developed which are not a threat to dolphins.

A POWERFUL WEAPON

More and more companies are being forced to label their goods so that the customer can tell if they are made in a safe way. Consumer pressure is a powerful weapon in making companies behave responsibly.

Right: A 'Dolphin Safe' label is stuck to cans containing tuna caught in the new way.

Below: Consumers can force industry to change by not buying products which harm the environment.

We all need to consider our lifestyles and buying habits. Not only do we need to try harder to buy products that are environmentally-sensitive, we also need to cut down on the amount we consume.

In the last 200 years, industry has proved that it can be very clever in coming up quickly with new ideas and inventions. In the difficult job of balancing the good things business and industry can bring with the bad, everybody has a role. Governments can use laws and taxes to cut pollution and exploitation. Consumers have power too. If we make it clear that we will only buy safe, clean products, industry will have to ensure that is what it makes.

Some of the world's most important inventions have come from industry. Now the challenge is to use those skills to develop technologies which will help preserve the planet.

GLOSSARY

atmosphere: the air, made up of the different gases that surround the earth.

Agenda 21: plan of action made at 1992 UN Conference on Environment and Development in an effort to preserve the earth's resources.

CFC: man-made gases used in aerosols and fridges which damage the ozone layer.

conservation: the protection of the environment and resources.

consumers: people who buy and use goods.

developed country: a country that relies on money from industry and in which factories provide more jobs than agriculture.

developing country: a country that relies on money from agriculture, rather than on manufacturing goods for export, for example.

emissions: harmful gases released into the air by factories and transport.

environment: describes all the conditions that surround us, such as the air, the soil and water; it provides the habitat for humans, other animals and plants.

freight: large amounts of goods transported on ships, lorries and trains.

fuels: natural and man-made products, such as coal and petrol, used to produce power.

landfill sites: large holes in the ground where rubbish and waste are buried.

non-renewable: anything that can only be used once.

pollution: waste products which damage the environment.

renewable: anything which can be used again and again without wasting valuable resources of the earth.

resources: natural things in the earth which are essential for making products or energy, such as coal, tin, copper, iron and oil.

supplier: a firm or person who provides an important service or item for a bigger company.

sustainable development: in this instance, to be able to maintain lifestyles or preserve resources over a long period of time.

taxes: money paid by people or companies to the government in order to fund services such as education, hospitals and roads for the good of the community.

toxic: poisonous.

the West: a term used to describe the world's richest countries, most of which are in Europe or the western half of the world.

FURTHER INFORMATION

Business in the Environment
5 Cleveland Place
London SW1Y 6JJ, UK
Tel: (0171) 321 6430

Friends of the Earth
26-28 Underwood Street
London N1 7JQ, UK
Tel: (0171) 490 1555

Greenpeace
Canonbury Villas
London N1 2PN, UK
Tel (0171) 865 8100

Oxfam
274 Banbury Road
Oxford OX2 7DZ, UK
Tel: (01865) 311311

**World Business Council
for Sustainable Development**
160 Route de Florissant
CH-1231 Conches
Geneva, SWITZERLAND
Tel: (00) 41 22 839 3100

**Business and Executive
Advisor Services**
Level 7/15 Young Street
Sydney, NSW 2000
AUSTRALIA
Tel: (02) 9241 4075

Department of Fair Trading
1 Fitz William Street
Parramatta, NSW 2150
AUSTRALIA
Tel: (02) 9895 0111

Greenpeace Australia
41 Holt Street
Surry Hills, NSW 2010
AUSTRALIA
Tel: (02) 9211 4066

Friends of the Earth
15/104 Bathurst Street
Sydney, NSW 2000
AUSTRALIA
Tel: (02) 9283 2004

INDEX